Originally published in 1900
by Houghton, Mifflin and Company, Boston and New York

First Greenwood Reprinting 1968
Second Greenwood Reprinting 1971

Library of Congress Catalogue Card Number 68-19293

ISBN 0-8371-0207-3

Printed in the United States of America

TO

K. R.

I DEDICATE THIS BOOK

THE INGERSOLL LECTURESHIP

Extract from the will of Miss Caroline Haskell Ingersoll, who died in Keene, County of Cheshire, New Hampshire, Jan. 26, 1893.

First. In carrying out the wishes of my late beloved father, George Goldthwait Ingersoll, as declared by him in his last will and testament, I give and bequeath to Harvard University in Cambridge, Mass., where my late father was graduated, and which he always held in love and honor, the sum of Five thousand dollars ($5,000) as a fund for the establishment of a Lectureship on a plan somewhat similar to that of the Dudleian lecture, that is — one lecture to be delivered each year, on any convenient day between the last day of May and the first day of December, on this subject, "the Immortality of Man," said lecture not to form a part of the usual college course, nor to be delivered by any Professor or Tutor as part of his usual routine of instruction, though any such Professor or Tutor may be appointed to such service. The choice of said lecturer is not to be limited to any one religious denomination, nor to any one profession, but may be that of either clergyman or layman, the appointment to take place at least six months before the delivery of said lecture. The above sum to be safely invested and three fourths of the annual interest thereof to be paid to the lecturer for his services and the remaining fourth to be expended in the publishment and gratuitous distribution of the lecture, a copy of which is always to be furnished by the lecturer for such purpose. The same lecture to be named and known as "the Ingersoll lecture on the Immortality of Man."

THE CONCEPTION OF
IMMORTALITY

I

 MAY as well begin this discussion by pointing out where, to my mind, lies the most central problem concerning man's immortality. In the real world in which our common-sense metaphysic believes, some things are obviously transient, and others, as, for instance, matter and the laws of nature, are more enduring, and perhaps (so common sense would nowadays tell us), are absolutely permanent. But permanence is of two sorts. A *type* may be permanent, — a law, a relationship. Thus the Binomial Theorem remains always true; and water continues to run down hill just as it did during the earliest geological periods. Or

that may be permanent which we usually
call an *individual* being. This particle of
matter, as, for instance, an individual atom,
or again, the individual whole called the
entire mass of matter of the universe, may
be permanent. Now when we ask about
the Immortality of Man, it is the permanence of the Individual Man concerning
which we mean to inquire, and not primarily the permanence of the human type,
as such, nor the permanence of any other
system of laws or relationships. So far
then, as to the mere statement of our
issue, I suppose that we are all agreed.

But in philosophy we who study any of
these fundamental problems are unwilling
to assert anything about a given subject,
unless we first understand what we mean
by that subject. Philosophy turns altogether upon trying to find out what our
various fundamental ideas mean. Thus,
when in practical life, you act dutifully, you
may not be wholly clear as to just what you
mean by your duty; but when you study

Moral Philosophy, your primal question is, What does the very Idea of Duty mean? Now precisely so, in case of the Immortality of the Individual Man, the question arises, What do we mean when we talk of an individual man at all? But this question, to my mind, is not a mere preliminary to an inquiry concerning immortality, but it includes by far the larger part of just that inquiry itself. For unless we know what an individual man is, we have no business even to raise the question whether he is immortal. But, on the other hand, if we can discover what we mean by an individual man, the very answer to that question will take us so far into the heart of things, and will imply so much as to our views about God, the World, and Man's place in the world, that the question about the immortality of man will become, in great measure, a mere incident in the course of this deeper discussion.

Accordingly, I shall here raise, and for the larger part of this lecture shall pursue,

an inquiry concerning what we mean by an Individual Man. Only towards the end of this discussion shall we come clearly to see that in defining the Individual Man, we have indeed been defining his Immortality.

The question as to the nature of an individual man is at once a problem of logic and an issue of life. I shall have to consider the matter in both aspects. In the first aspect our question becomes identical with the problem, What is it that makes *any* real being an individual? This question is a very ancient, and if you choose commonplace one, which has been studied from time to time ever since Aristotle. I can give you small insight, in my brief time, into its complications; and what I needs must say about it may appear very formal and dreary. But like all the central problems of Logic, this one really pulsates with all the mystery of life; and before I am done, I shall hope to give you a glimpse of the sense in which this is true. Such a glimpse will become possible as

soon as I apply the logical question about individuals to the case of the individual man.   That all men including yourself are more or less mysterious beings to you, you are already aware.   What I want to show you is that the chief mystery about any man is precisely the mystery of his individual nature, i. e., of the nature whereby he is this man and no other man.   I want to show you that the only solution of this mystery lies in conceiving every man as so related to the world and to the very life of God, that in order to be an individual at all a man has to be very much nearer to the Eternal than in our present life we are accustomed to observe.   So much then for an outline of our enterprise.   And now for its inevitably complicated details.[1]

II

WE all naturally believe that the real world about us contains individual things. And if you ask what we naturally mean by believing this, I first reply, apart from any more formal definition of individuality, by saying that we believe our world to consist of facts, of realities, which are all ultimately different from one another, and unlike one another, by virtue of precisely what constitutes their very existence as facts or as realities. Things may resemble one another as much as you will. But deeper than their resemblance has to be, according to our common-sense view, the fact that they are still somehow individually or numerically different beings. Yonder lights, for instance, are in your present opinion all of them different from one an-

other, despite their resemblances as luminous objects. You and your neighbors are different beings. And such individual difference, as you hold, enters very deeply into your inmost constitution, or into the constitution of any person or thing in the universe. No matter how much two people, say twins, look alike, talk alike, think alike, or feel alike, we still hold that they are different beings ; and we naturally hold that this difference lies somehow deeper than do all their resemblances, inner or outer. For that each one of them is, or that he is this being, depends upon and implies the fact that he is nobody else ; and just as neither of the twins could have any appearance, or voice, or thoughts, or feelings at all unless he first existed ; just so, too, neither of them, as the individual that he is, could exist at all unless he were *this* person, and *not* the other. So that to exist implies, as we usually hold, to be different from the rest of the world of existences. And since I must exist if I am to

have any qualities whereby I can resemble another being, and must differ from all other beings if I am to exist, it naturally seems that my difference from all the rest of the world is, in a sense, the deepest truth about me. However little I may know about myself, common sense therefore supposes me to be at least very sure that I am nobody else, and so am different from anybody else.

By an individual, then, we mean an essentially unique being, or a being such that there exists, and can exist, but one of the type constituted by this individual being.

An easy task it is then, although indeed a very dry and abstract task, to tell what in general constitutes *individuality*, if we take the term simply as an abstract noun. For the beings of the world are made individuals by whatever truly serves to distinguish each of them from all the rest, to keep them, as it were, seemingly apart in their Being. But now, if we leave this barely

abstract statement, and come closer to the facts of life, I may next point out that, if individuality in general is easily defined, this *individual*, precisely in so far as it is an unique being, is from the nature of the case peculiarly hard to characterize, or to explain, or to conceive, or to define, or to observe, or in any other way to know. In fact, when we look closer we soon see that our human thought is able to define only types of beings, and never individuals, so that *this individual* is always for us indefinable.   On the other hand our human sense experience shows us only *kinds* of sensory impressions, and never unique objects as unique.

For now there comes to our attention a very commonplace, but important fact, regarding the process of our knowledge. We have so far accepted the natural view that the differences of various existent things lie at the basis, so to speak, of all resemblances. But whenever we know anything, we are dependent upon taking

account at once, and in one act, of both likenesses and differences. These two aspects of facts are somewhat differently related to our consciousness ; but we never really come to know a difference without in some wise either reducing to or consciously relating it to a likeness. One of the lights that you see differs, to your mind, from another light in size, in brightness, or in place. Yet just because you see them thus differing, all of them for that very reason are seen as in the same larger place, viz., in this room, or as alike in all being bright, or as alike in all having size. Thus, whenever you clearly see wherein they are different, say in brightness, size, place, you also see how, in just this same respect in which they differ, they also have some resemblances to one another. This fact, that you always know likenesses and differences at once, or in one act, makes it impossible to sift out in your knowledge all the resemblances of your world, and to put them in one place

by themselves, in your mind, while you
put all the differences in another place.
For the likenesses stick to the differences,
and always come away with them, when
you try to analyze your world, even in the
most abstract thinking process. Just as
some of the miner's gold washes away in
the tailings, and just as some of the ac-
companying substances that a chemist tries
to remove by a particular process of dis-
tillation may distill over with whatever
was to be separated from them, so too,
when, in your discriminating observation,
or in your abstract thinking, you try, for
the purposes of your analysis, to wash the
resemblances out of the facts, and to keep
the differences, or to distill off the individuality of the different things, you find
that always resemblance stubbornly clings
to difference, and *vice versa*. Nor do our
figures of the tailings and the distillations
give quite an adequate idea of the actual
hopelessness of trying to separate in our
consciousness, for purposes of analysis, the

like and the different aspects of our observed world.   For, in our knowledge, the
consciousness of likeness and the consciousness of difference help each other ;
and therefore in a measure, it is true that
the more we get of one of them, before our
knowledge, the more we get of the other.
So they decline altogether to be known
separately.   Thus, only pretty closely sim-
ilar objects can seem to us to stand, from
our point of view, in an observably sharp
contrast to one another.   We can see the
contrast only when we also see the close
similarity.   For instance, it is much easier
to be aware of a definite difference or contrast between two poets than it is to be
conscious of the difference or contrast between a poet and a blackberry or a para-
bola.   Whenever we clearly see what a
difference is, there we also observe a likeness, and the difference and the likeness,
as seen, always relate to the same aspects
of the objects.

   This being the fashion of our know-

ledge, one sees at once how hard it must
be for knowledge either to find in the impressions of sense, or to define by thought,
just wherein one thing ultimately differs
from all other things. An individual being,
as we have seen, is thought by our common
sense to be, first of all, different from any
other being. We try either to say or to
see wherein it thus differs, or what constitutes its individuality. Forthwith we only
the more clearly see and state and conceive
points wherein it not only differs from all
other objects, but also, and at the same
time, resembles them. This is the fate of
our knowing process, and therefore, whenever we observe closely, all individuality
seems to be conceived and observed by us
as merely relative. Individuality is known
to us only as an aspect inseparable from
what is not individuality. But just because
a thing, according to our natural view, is to
be an individual to the very heart and core
of its existence, it seems that, if we are to be
able to see or to express this individuality,

we ought somewhere to be able to find or to conceive the individuality of each thing as a fact by itself, — as a difference, deeper than all resemblances, ideally separable from them, and not merely bound up in this inseparable way with them, or dependent upon them. Hence we always fail when we try to describe any individual exhaustively.

Morcover, still another aspect of our difficulty often occurs to our minds, and is especially baffling. Anything is an individual in so far as it genuinely differs not only from any other existent being, but from any other being that is genuinely possible or that is rightly conceivable. You, for instance, if you are a real individual, are such that nobody else, whether actual or possible, could ever share your individual nature, or be rightly confounded with you. Now, however closely we observe, and no matter how carefully we conceive, a thing, we at best only observe or conceive actual likenesses and differences

between this thing and other present or remembered things. We can never either see or abstractly think just how or why it is that no other possible thing could possess the characters, whatever they are, which we have once noticed or have actually found this thing to possess. Suppose, for instance, that I see the color of an object. So far I in no sense see why other objects might not possess just that color. In general other objects do. So colors are not purely individual characteristics of things. Suppose, however, that I see a hundred autumn leaves, and sorting them, find indeed that no two of them are precisely alike in shading and in detail of coloring. In that case I at first seem to be finding what is individual in each leaf. But no. For so far I have only seen actual likenesses and differences; and so far only my present autumn leaves are indeed seen to be different. But I have not seen why there might not be in the world, unseen as yet by me, other autumn leaves

precisely like any particular one of these leaves in every detail of coloring that I have noticed. Hence I have not yet taken note, in any leaf, of a coloring such as could not possibly be repeated somewhere else in the forest; and therefore I have not yet actually observed what it is that constitutes the truly individual existence of any one of the leaves. For whatever is a truly individual character of any existent thing is a character that simply could not be shared by another thing ; and whatever makes you an existent individual being forbids anybody else, whether actual or possible, to be possessed of precisely your individual characteristics.

Historians and biographers try to tell us about individuals. Do they ever actually succeed in getting before us the adequate description of any one individual as such ? No. *Man* you can define ; but the true essence of any man, say, for instance, of Abraham Lincoln, remains the endlessly elusive and mysterious object of the bio-

grapher's interest, of the historian's comments, of popular legend, and of patriotic devotion.   There is no adequate definition or description of Abraham Lincoln just in so far as he was the unique individual.

And why, I once more ask, is this so? Why can you not tell all that constitutes the individual what he is?   One answer, I insist, lies just here.   Suppose that you had overcome all the other limitations that hinder the biographer or the historian from knowing the facts about his hero. Suppose that you had a description or definition say of Abraham Lincoln, and suppose you assumed this definition or description to be an exact and exhaustive one.   The definition would mention, perhaps, the physical appearance and bearing of Lincoln, the traits of his character, the secrets of his success, and whatever else you may choose to regard as characteristic of him.   Well, suppose the definition finished.   The question might be raised, at once, Is it possible, is it conceivable,

that the world should contain another man
who embodied just that now defined type,
— who looked, spoke, thought, felt, com-
manded, and succeeded as Lincoln the
War President did ? If you answer,
"No ;" then we may at once retort, How
can you know that only one man of this or
of any once defined type can exist ? Have
you the secret of creation ? Is every man's
mould shattered (to use the familiar meta-
phor) when the man is made ? And if so,
how come you to be aware of the fact ?
But if you answer, "Yes ; more than one
man of this defined type is at least possible, or conceivable ;" then equally well
we may point out that hereby you merely
admit that you have *not* yet defined what
makes Abraham Lincoln different from
any and from all other men, actual or possible.   For if the possible men, fashioned
after the likeness that your definition has
expounded, were to come into existence,
no one of these other men would be, in
your opinion, Abraham Lincoln himself, or

be entitled to his honors or his merits. They would differ from him by precisely the whole breadth of their individuality. They would have no right to his property, no share in his individual fame, and no hope, so to speak, of becoming worthy to take his place upon the Judgment Day. Yet, by hypothesis, they would conform to whatever definition of him you had once given as an adequate characterization of his type.

You may here interpose, if you will, by saying that all such idle suppositions about the possible reduplications of the type of Abraham Lincoln are worthless, since the practically interesting question is whether men whose identity runs any risk of being confounded with that of the great President exist or are to be found; and this question, according to our common view, is easily to be answered in the negative. But my present interest, in mentioning the possible cases of other representatives of Lincoln's once defined type, lies merely

in showing that whatever the individuality of anything really is, we men never adequately come to know wherein it consists, and so I here point out that while you are doubtless somehow quite sure of Lincoln's individuality, of his unexampled uniqueness, you have not positively defined wherein that uniqueness and individuality consists, until your definition has actually expressed *why*, or at least *how* it is that there *can be no other* man of his type.   So long as you merely appeal then to human experience to show that there *is* no other such man to be found, our present argument remains untouched.

But even if we passed back again to experience to help us, we should still find once more, as we found in case of the autumn leaves, that no experience can show us the unique.   The facts of sense are essentially sorts of experience, — characters, types, — fashions of feelings.   Uniqueness as such is thus precisely what I can never directly find present to my senses.

When you first learn from the logic text-
books or from Aristotle that the individual
is the indefinable, you are indeed fain with
Aristotle to turn back to experience, as we
just attempted to do in case of Abraham
Lincoln. You are disposed to say that
the individual is the proper object of sense.
But Aristotle himself knew better than to
rest content in this view. As he already
saw, sense also, in its own way, brings to
our consciousness only the more or less
vaguely general, or at best the typical, —
not the unique.[2]

The very young children trust their
senses for guidance, in the use of their
earliest language at the time when they
name every object by its vaguely observed
type. So, perhaps, they name all men
alike "papa," or for a while they call all
animals " dogs," or identify cows as "cats,"
or use any other of the delightful confu-
sions that characterize the first year of
speech. Sense and feeling, taken as directly present experience, supply us only

with general types, and, apart from other motives, guide us only to general ideas, never to a direct knowledge of individuals.

You see then, in sum, that our human type of knowledge never shows us existent individuals as being truly individual. Sense, taken by itself, shows us merely sense qualities, — colors, sounds, odors, tastes.   These are general characters. Abstract thinking defines for us types. A discriminating comparison of many present objects of experience, such as autumn leaves, or human faces, or handwritings, shows us manifold differences, but always along with and subject to the presence of likenesses, so that we never find what common sense assumes to exist, namely, such a difference between any individual and all the rest of the world as lies deeper than every resemblance.   And even if by comparisons and discriminations we had found how one being appears to differ from all other now existent beings, we should not yet have seen what it is that distinguishes

each individual being from all possible beings. Yet such a difference from all possible beings is presupposed when you talk, for instance, of your own individuality.

III

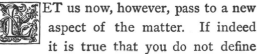ET us now, however, pass to a new aspect of the matter. If indeed it is true that you do not define in your thought, or empirically observe through any direct experience of your senses, that the world consists of unique individual beings, then we are next disposed to say that the dogma of common sense upon this subject is the result of some very recondite interpretation of your experience. But if we ask whence we came by this interpretation, I must call your attention to that region of your life where you are indeed surest of the individuality of the facts, and most familiar with its meaning. This region is that of your intimate human relationships. Your family and your nearest friends are indeed for your human faith and loyalty

through and through individuals. You are
sure of their uniqueness. You resist most
decidedly the hypothesis that what for you
constitutes the essence of their individuality could conceivably be shared, like the
characters of a mere type, by other beings
in the world. "There is no other child
quite like my child, — no other love quite
like my love, — no other friend wholly like
this friend, — no other home the precise
possible substitute for this home " — how
familiar and human such assertions are.
Now this affirmation of the uniqueness
of our own, and of those to whom our
hearts belong, has something about it that
obviously goes beyond both sense and
abstract thinking. It expresses itself
in quite absolute terms. Meanwhile it
is much warmer and more vital than the
before-mentioned colorless assumption that
all the real beings in the world are in some
wise unique beings, or that the universe is
made up of individuals. Yet this present
and more vital assertion seems to express

the very inmost spirit of intimacy of personal loyalty.   And meanwhile it is, in its implications, quite as metaphysical as is the most general theory of any philosopher. For I must still insist, — not even in case of our most trusted friends, — not even after years of closest intimacy, — no, not even in the instance of Being that lies nearest to each one of us, — not even in the consciousness that each one of us has of his own Self, — can we men as we now are either define in thought or find directly presented in our experience the individual beings whom we most of all love and trust, or most of all presuppose. and regard, as somehow certainly real.   For even within the circle of your closest intimacies our former rule holds true, that, if you attempt to define by your thought the unique, it transforms itself into an unsatisfactory abstraction, — a type and not a person, — a mere fashion of possible existence, that might as well be shared by a legion as confined to the case of a single being.   And

just so, too, the other previous result ob-
tains, namely, that when you try to find the
certainly unique even in your own house-
hold, it eludes your direct observation, for it
is a form of Being that belongs to a far higher
sphere than that of any merely immediate
experience.   It is just for this reason that
the individual object of your oldest friend-
ship is not merely a psychological problem
to you, but also a metaphysical mystery.
The real presence of your friend you may
indeed love with an exclusive affection that
forbids you to believe that any other could
take his unique place anywhere in the
whole realm of Being ; but you meet this
real presence of an individual never at any
time as a fact of sense.   Your doctrine
about this real presence of your friend remains in common life a dogma just as truly
as if it were a dogma of a supernatural
faith.   It is with the individual of daily
life as with the lady of Browning's lyric,
for whom the lover searches through
"room after room" of the house they
" inhabit together :" —

" Yet the day wears,
   And door succeeds door ;
   I try the fresh fortune —
   Range the wide house from the wing to the centre —
   Still the same chance !   She goes out as I enter ! "

And now, if you ask why this lady is thus elusive, I answer, because she is an individual.   And an individual is a being that no finite search can find.

As for yourself, you notoriously are such that the Self is, and is a real individual. But who amongst us defines by his abstract statement of his own type, or finds by dwelling upon his familiar masses of mere organic sensation, what his own unique Self may be ?   Or who amongst us conceives himself in his uniqueness except as the remote goal of some ideal process of coming to himself and of awakening to the truth about his own life ?   Only an infinite process can show me who I am.

On the other hand, when we dwell upon these cases that lie nearest to our vital interests, we do indeed begin to find out the

deeper meaning of something that in the
instances formerly mentioned seemed to
be a matter for cold and curious logical
inquiry. We begin to find out, namely,
the deeper meaning of this our so fixed,
and yet at first sight so arbitrary assumption that our real world, despite the imperfections of our conception and the vague
generality of our direct experience, does
consist of individuals.   For in case of the
objects of our nearer and of our more consciously exclusive affections, we are often
well aware how arbitrary our mere speech
about the experienced or defined uniqueness of these objects of affection must
seem to any external observer.   We rec-
ognize this apparent arbitrariness of our
description of the unique object ; but we
even glory therein.   We confess that we cannot tell wherein our friend is so individual.
We emphasize the confession. We make it
a deliberate topic of portrayal in art. And
what we feel, as we do this, is that this arbitrary speech of ours is a sign that we are

pursuing a very precious secret, which nobody else has the right to share. Herein we find a hint also of a certain ideal view of the innermost nature of Being, — a view which simply cannot be translated into the language of abstract description, or adequately embodied in the materials of present sensation ; but a view which is all the truer for that very reason.   For this view the Real is indeed something beyond our present human sense and our descriptive science. The individuals are, as we are sure, the most real facts of our world.   But yet there is for us, as for Browning's lover, something endlessly fascinating about our hopeless human inability to show to anybody else, or to verify by even our own immediate experience, just in what way they are thus so individual.   This our finite situation has its own perplexing and beautiful irony. We rise above our helplessness even as we confess it ; for this helplessness hints to us that our real world is behind the veil.

The inner nature, the true Being of

these beloved individuals about us and of
our own individuality within, thus constitutes, so to speak, the genuinely and whole-
somely occult aspect of our most commonplace life. That we are really in the most
intimate relations with this so familiar, and
precious, and yet so occult world, where in
truth our most intimate friends and our
actual selves even now dwell, we are sure.
But that the gates seem barred whenever
we try to penetrate or to reveal the truth
of this very world, — this is something so
baffling, so stimulating, and yet in a way
so absurd, that in our lighter moments we
find our own incapacity to make our world
manifest to our human vision endlessly
amusing. And the play with these mysteries constitutes a great part of the poetic
arts. It is, I must insist, merely a concrete
instance of the fundamental logical and
metaphysical problem as to how the world
can consist of individuals.

To mention a familiar instance. All the
world loves a lover, and, in a sense, loves

in sympathy with him. Yet nearly all the
faithful lovers are certain profoundly to
disagree with him as to the most central
article of his faith. For he loves an individual, unique, without a peer, — one who
is most lovable just because she occupies
a place that no other could take. They,
— the other faithful lovers, — each one of
them also loves a peerless individual. And
therefore they all have to use indeed very
nearly the same formulas whenever they
try to tell why they love. But they all
disagree, just because they apply their
creeds to different objects. They all describe essentially the same type, namely,
the perfect woman. They differ about her
identity. Or if they do not thus disagree —
then, to be sure, a tragedy is in the mak-
ing. In the endless disagreement of the
lovers lies their only hope of harmony.

Now the problem as to the worthy object of love is precisely, and, as I myself
maintain, philosophically, identical with
the logical problem as to what constitutes

an individual being.[3]   Whom shall one
love ?   The unique object.   There shall
be no other like the beloved.   But for
what characters shall one choose the beloved ?   For *mere* uniqueness, for *mere* oddi-
ties as such ?   No.   For perfections, for ex-
cellencies, for ideally valuable qualities, is
the beloved rightly chosen, and not other-
wise.   Be it so, then.   The lover, if justi-
fied in his love, believes not only that his
beloved is different from all other beings,
but also that she is in some wise more ex-
cellent than all others.   This great faith,
if sincere, longs for expression.   One must
praise the beloved ; or if one is no poet,
one must look abroad to find the already
written words with which to praise her.
But in what language shall the praise be
expressed ?   In human speech of general
meaning, known and understood by all
men.   But the qualities that the lover finds
in his own unique beloved, when once expressed in this common speech of men,
become in large measure identical with

the qualities that all the beloved women
of the world have been said, by the poets
and the lovers, to possess. Of course there
are those well known differences in types
of recognized perfection, which have to do
with color of eyes, and with other features,
but on the whole, the lover in expressing,
in defining, if you will, the perfections of
his love, has merely described with minor
variations one type, — and, thank Heaven,
an extremely general and universally well
known type, — the type of all the beloved
women.   In other words, he has set forth
every real or apparent noble quality of his
beloved except precisely what makes her
unique.   Yet his loyalty still earnestly in-
sists that he loves her for nothing so much
as for that she *is* unique, and is even
thereby quite unlike all the other beloved
women.

Hereupon the logician must become a
little suspicious of the lover. The lover
says that he loves but One. Yet when
he tells about her he describes a type.

Does he then really love only the type?
For, alas, his poetic accounts are but general. Just when he describes his love—
"So careful of the type he seems, — so
careless of the single life." But no, this
thought is an insult to loyal love. True
love is indeed essentially careful of the single life. Yet is it then truly the unique
being that one loves? Alas! if this is true,
why then does the lover's halting speech,
when it praises, describe absolutely nothing
whatever but the type? The beloved, if
logically disposed, may even notice this, the
pathetic irony of our human loyalty. "You
might have said all this," she may retort,
— "you might have said all this to any
other woman who merely happened to please
you."

Now in vain would the lover attempt
adequately to reply that the beloved is indeed, as a matter of mere experience, sufficiently different in face and carriage from
all the other observable people to be capable of what we usually call identification,

so that, for instance, the postman or the teller at the bank also no doubt recognizes her face when he sees it, and practically confuses her with nobody else. For the ground of loyal love is not meant to be simply the same as this practical ground that we use for purposes of ordinary identification. The lover does not mean that his beloved is merely capable of being identified. It is true that these facts of experience, these observed differences of face and manner, become, from the first, lighted up for the lover's appreciation with all the beauty of devotion, and so blend in his experience of affection with his sense of loyalty. That is so far as it should be. He loves indeed also the face and the voice, but for the sake of their unique owner. Yet the very question that before seemed to us a very formal matter of logic would become, if once raised, a very practical question for love. I do not advise anybody to raise it in any particular case. But, as a mere matter now of theory: If there were

found in the world another with just such
a face, voice, bearing, and other outward
seeming and inward sentiment as the beloved, would the lover not merely by chance
confuse the two, through his mortal ignorance, but actually and knowingly love both
of them at once and equally ? If he must
answer, " Yes," then indeed, whatever his
protestations, he loves not the real individual. There is then no true loyalty in his
love. He is fond of a mere type.

But if he loves the individual, then indeed he could bear the easy test that, in
the Hindu poem of Nala and Damayanti,
the gods apply to the princess of the story.
For when, in that story, the princess, by
virtue of the privilege belonging to her
rank, is about to choose her lover from
amongst the suitors, assembled upon a
solemn occasion to hear her decision, four
of the gods, to please their high caprice,
stand beside the real lover, whom the princess has already in her heart chosen.
Each god assumes precisely the real lov-

er's guise and seeming. The princess finds
then before her five men, all absolutely
alike, and all fashioned exactly as is the
man of her heart. In her perplexity she
wonders a brief moment ; but then, per-
ceiving in her mind the heavenly wiles,
she lifts up her voice in humble prayer
that those of the group who arc *not* the
right one may be pleased to behave a little
more like gods, that she may see more
clearly to choose her own. The gods re-
lent, and obey. But the princess, as she
thus finds her mortal lover, hereby shows
us also somewhat more clearly what our
loyal consciousness of the nature of an individual means. It means that for our
Will, however sense deceives, and however
ill thought defines, there *shall be* none precisely like the beloved. And just herein,
namely, in this voluntary choice, in this ac-
tive postulate, lies our essential consciousness of the true nature of individuality.
Individuality is something that we demand
of our world, but that, in this present realm

of experience, we never find. It is the object of our purposes, but not now of our attainment; of our intentions, but not of their present fulfillment; of our will, but not of our sense nor yet of our abstract thought; of our rational appreciation, but not of our description ; of our love, but not of our verbal confession. We pursue it with the instruments of a thought and of an art that can define only types, and of a form of experience that can show us only instances and generalities. The unique eludes us ; yet we remain faithful to the ideal of it ; and in spite of sense and of our merely abstract thinking, it becomes for us the most real thing in the actual world, although for us it is the elusive goal of an infinite quest.[4]

And therefore it is that the lovers join in reporting the same things of all whom they love; yet in meaning, nevertheless, wholly different beings by their speech. Therefore it is that the soldiers in Bayard Taylor's Sebastopol lyric, as they sing

in the trenches, before they storm the fort, try to confess each the tearful secret of his own heart, as he thinks of home, but they do so in words that are the same for all of them : —

> " Each heart recalled a different name,
> But all sang Annie Laurie."

The true individuals are thus not seen by us, not described by us. But in our more intimate life we love individuals, we will to pursue them and to be loyal to them. Love and loyalty never directly find their unique objects, but remain faithful to them although unseen.

IV

WE have so far dealt both with various negative aspects of this idea of individuality and also with its positive significance for life. We must now ask, Is there any truth in this idea of individuality? Are we in any sense right in regarding our world as one where there are these unique individuals whom we mortals can define only in terms of our will to seek them, and can conceive only as the goal of an essentially ideal process?

The adequate answer to this question as to the real Being of an individual would involve, as I have confessed from the very outset, an entire system of philosophy. Shall I venture here merely to hint the grounds upon which I think that we have a right at least to attempt just such primal problems? This idea of the individuality

of all things is, in my own opinion, an idea
not merely of the emotional interest now
illustrated.   It is also an idea without
which, in the end, all serious science is impossible.   For science too, although not
sentimental, is itself a loyal expression of
an essentially practical interest in final, i. e.,
in individual truth.   Science, if unable to
describe or to find the unique, everywhere
postulates its existence as the goal of a
process of inquiry.   And this idea of the
individual is an idea that directs all con-
duct of our intellect in the presence of our
experience.   To believe anywhere in genuine reality is to believe in individuality.
In every special science that deals with
either nature or man, you will find, then,
if you look closer, that in some form the
concept and the problem of the individual
enters in a fashion less sentimental indeed
than is the lover's problem, but quite as
insistent, quite as baffling, both for our
empirical search and for our abstract definitions, and quite as suggestive that if our

world has reality, this reality is one which no finite process of finding and defining can exhaust. Quite impossible is it, however, to decline to face this problem upon the supposed grounds that the ultimate nature of real things is once for all unknowable. The conception of reality itself is precisely as much an expression of our human needs and purposes, as is the conception of a steam engine or of a political party ; and if the conception so far baffles us, that is because we have not yet looked deeply enough into the life out of which this very conception of the real world of individuals springs. Let us then inquire a little more searchingly. To be sure, for this inquiry there is here no adequate space. I can give only a bare hint of an idealistic interpretation of the real world. Elsewhere I have tried to state in explicit form the argument now to be barely indicated. Regard what follows, if you will, not as any attempt at proof, but as a mere summary.

We have up to this point spoken of the relation of the concept of the individual to the direct experience of sense, and to the abstract definitions of the intellect. We have found that neither of these could furnish to us an adequate expression of the nature of an individual. We have also seen, in speaking of the more vital aspects of our problem, that an individual, if not describable, is still sincerely intended or willed as the object of a devotion that, in us, can only express itself as the endless pursuit of a goal. The natural statement of our problem becomes then this: Do these endless pursuits of ideal goals, in terms of which we define our relation to the undefinable individual beings whom we love, or whom in science we seek to know, —do these ideal pursuits, I say, correspond to a truth anywhere expressed beyond us? Is reality in its wholeness a realm of Purpose, rather than merely of observable finite facts and of abstractly definable characters?

As to the most general answer to this question, I must indeed first respond that, for the reasons now illustrated, I hold the concept of individuality to be not merely from our human point of view, but in itself, essentially and altogether, a teleological concept, — a concept implying that the facts of any world where there really are individuals express will and purpose. Suppose a being not now a man, but a being as far above our mere poverty of conscious life as you please, yet a being whose whole life consists merely of sense contents, or of mere facts of immediate feeling, — colors, forms, tastes, touches, pleasures, and pains. Such a being could indeed observe. But he would never observe individuals as individuals. On the other hand, suppose any purely intelligent being, whose mind was full of mere ideas, i. e., of patterns, types, schemes, class conceptions, definitions. Such a being, however wise in his own way, could never know individual facts as such. He might know laws,

orders of truth, systems of necessary valid-
ity ; but if his world contained individual
facts, he would never know this to be true.
He would be, for instance, by our hypothesis, himself an individual, for we have
just spoken of him as such ; but he would
never be able to know himself as this individual.   With the proverbial absent-mind-
edness of the abstractly wise, this supposed
pure intelligence would be quite unaware
that he himself, or that anybody else, possessed individuality.   He would be loyal
to no individual objects.   His world would
be for him a collection of disembodied
theorems, and of mere possibilities.

And now, even if you suppose the being
of mere experience with whom we just be-
gan, to acquire all the wisdom of the other
being, the supposed abstract thinker ; still,
even this resulting being, who would be an
observer of ideal laws and of immediate
experiences, in this combination would
nevertheless not yet find true individuality
in his world.   His world would now be one

where there were types and feelings; but still not one where unique beings were observed to be real.

But next suppose a being whose world not merely shows him contents of feeling and types of law, but also expresses his will, and not merely expresses this will, but satisfies it. Suppose that this being finds in his world, namely, all that his love and all that his wisdom seek. This being will observe his world as embodiment of his plans, as an exhaustive presentation of his will and purpose. Now this being can indeed say: "This world and *no other* is my world, for these facts and *no others* are what I want, just because in these facts my purposes are satisfied." For the satisfied will is precisely the will that seeks no other embodiment. Now such a being, and such a being only, would be aware of the uniqueness of his facts, and so would know individuals as individuals.

The very conception, then, of an individual as a real being, precisely because it is

no abstract conception, but is rather the conception of a unique being, is one that no pure thought or experience can express, but is a conception expressible only in terms of a satisfied will. An individual is a being that adequately expresses a purpose. Or again, an individual so expresses a purpose that no other being can take the place of this individual as an expression of this purpose. And the sole test of this sort of uniqueness lies in the fact that in this individual being, just in so far as its type gets expression at all, the will or purpose which it expresses rests content with it, desires no other, will have no other.

I conclude then, so far, that if this world contains real individuals at all, it is a teleological world, and a world that not only expresses purpose, but completely and adequately expresses a purpose precisely in so far as it contains real individuals.

Nor need this result be interpreted merely with reference to the more sentimental illustrations used a moment since.

The purposes which various individuals express may be those of science, or those of human love, — those of our warmer passions, or those of our calmer reason, — those of man, or those of God. Any of these various purposes, or all of them at once, may win a place in Being. My whole case so far is that whether you talk of angels or atoms, your individual beings, if real at all, are real only as unique embodiments of purpose. And their uniqueness can only depend upon the fact that in each of them some will is so satisfied that it seeks and will have no other. Therefore it is indeed that loyal human love is in us the best example of an individuating principle. The love that will have no other than this beloved is our best hint of the sense in which purpose must be fulfilled in the world, if individuals are to be real at all.

Our question then becomes this: Does the real world fulfill purposes? Does it express will? Does it embody ideals in unique and satisfactory fulfillment? But

this question at once raises the most central issue of philosophy. In what sense is there any real world? What are its ultimate facts? What is Reality?[5]

The answer to these questions must be, like the questions, founded upon a desire to deal with first principles for their own sake. For the issue upon which depends every philosophical problem about the general order of the world is raised when one asks the question, What is a fact? We have said that the most significant facts, even of the world of common sense and of science, have aspects that transcend the limits of our direct human consciousness. But we have not said that such facts have no relation whatever to our own experience, but only that our human type of experience is very inadequate to exhaust their meaning, or to present them in their wholeness. In truth, our whole search after facts, our whole belief in the reality of the world, depends upon a recognition that our experience is inadequate to ex-

press the conscious purposes that we have in mind even when we scrutinize this our experience itself, to see what it contains. And our own philosophical argument will hold that in consequence you must define the whole Reality of things in terms of Purpose.

At any thinking moment of your human life, you inquire, you find yourself ignorant, you doubt, you wonder, or you investigate. Now as you do this you have present to your consciousness what are called, in the narrower sense of that term, ideas, — that is, ideas of objects **not** now present to you, and of objects that, if present, would answer your questions, settle your doubts, accomplish the end of your investigations. Now your ideas, as such, mean precisely certain thoughtful processes that are more or less consciously present in your momentary state of mind as you inquire. But the objects concerning which you inquire are, by hypothesis, not wholly present to you at the instant of your doubt or wonder. For

were they present, your inquiries would be
answered. They are viewed as absent; and
you also call them, taken, as it were, in
themselves, — you call them, I say, the
facts in the case. You conceive them,
usually, as in large measure independent of
your ideas. And yet the facts and your
ideas cannot be in truth wholly independent of each other as ordinary Realism assumes; for were they without any mutual
dependence whatever, how could the ideas
really have the facts as their objects? Or
how could it make any difference to the
ideas, as conscious processes, with an intent or purpose of their own, whether
the wholly independent facts agreed with
them, or not? Or yet again, to put the
same consideration in another form, the
ideas, if they have any bearing upon facts
at all, even if they simply express ignorance of the facts, or doubt about the facts,
or error regarding facts, or blunder, or
delusion, — yet still doubt, or error, or delusion about facts, which are really their

objects, — the ideas, I say, must in any such case stand in that seemingly so mysterious relation to the facts beyond them which is implied when we say, *The ideas are such as genuinely to mean the facts.* Even in your conscious ignorance, in doubt, in error, in delusion, if you really doubt, or err, or are deluded, your ideas, however fragmentary, are thus linked by the tie of objectively genuine meaning to the outer facts, however lofty or remote, concerning which you think and are therefore in one Whole of Meaning with those facts.

Now what does this genuine tie, called the meaning of an idea, this link by which the idea is bound to its seemingly external object, called the outer fact, — what, I ask, does this link imply? What is the true union between any idea and its object? The question as stated is absolutely general, is involved in every inquiry, in any sort of fact, and is therefore at issue whenever you consider the relation of any of your ideas, and so of yourself as the person

having these ideas, to facts whether physical or spiritual, to facts whether in a laboratory or in the eternal world, to facts whether in this room or in the remotest ages of time, to facts about your next friend, or to facts of God's mind or of immortality.   If, for instance, I now have a genuine idea of your minds while I speak to you, or if you have any idea really referring to my own mind, then our minds are actually and metaphysically linked by the ties of mutual meaning.   In other words, we are then not wholly sundered beings.   We are somehow more whole of meaning.   And if you now think of Sirius, or of the universe, then your idea, if it really means anything whatever that is objective, is in the same whole of meaning with your object.   But what constitutes this whole of meaning ?

The question has its especial difficulty in the fact that, in speaking of an idea and its object, just in so far as you sunder the two, and view them as mutually independ-

ent entities, you fail to see how the conscious idea can make any real reference to
that entity yonder, beyond it, and different
from it. For how should anybody, or how
should anybody's ideas, consciously refer
to an object that is still in no sense a part
of the consciousness which possesses the
idea? On the other hand, if the object to
which our ideas refer is simply itself one
of our own ideas, or is simply a fact present to our experience, — if, in other words,
idea and object are in my own unity of
consciousness together, then how should
an idea be able to err, as we constantly
find our own ideas erring, regarding their
objects? How, in brief, should ignorance
and error be at all possible?

To bring our whole problem then to a
single focus: When I think of outer existence, I think of something as not wholly
and just now consciously present to me;
and yet I think of myself as meaning this
something. My object is somehow here,
in my consciousness, — genuinely here;

and yet somehow not here, since I inquire
and perhaps err about it. Now how can I
thus mean to refer to more than my object
now present to my consciousness, while
still, in order thus to refer at all, I must
fix my attention upon some fact now present in my mind?

To all these fundamental questions philosophy, as I hold, must answer: I can refer
to any object beyond me solely by observ-
ing the inadequacy of my present and
passing conscious idea to its own conscious
purpose. I cannot directly look beyond
my own consciousness; but I pass beyond
my present solely by virtue of my will, my
intent, my dissatisfaction. But this very
will and dissatisfaction have my own present imperfection and inadequacy as their
direct object. And consequently, by the
object itself, by my real world, I can mean
nothing but that which in the end, despite
all my ignorance or error or finite misfor-
tune, somehow adequately fulfills my whole
will. Thus the very idea of a real being

is the idea of something that fulfills a purpose. What is thus thought of is indeed conceived as the outer object of an idea, and so as a fact beyond the idea, and yet meant by the idea. This relation of being beyond an idea, and yet meant by that idea, is, however, a possible relation, a relation that has any sense whatever only in so far, first, as the idea is an inadequate expression in our present human consciousness of its own purpose, and in so far, secondly, as the object meant stands related to the idea as that which fulfills the whole intent which is now partially expressed in the idea. And so we can indeed say, as Schopenhauer said, although not wholly in his sense, The real world is my Will.

In other words, to be, to exist, to be a fact, to be real, — any one of these expressions simply means, to express in wholeness the meaning that imperfect conscious ideas, such as we mortals have, now only partially express. To be, or to be a fact,

means then, not to be independent of finite
ideas, but to accomplish fully and finally
what they only intend, to present in wholeness what they only find in fragment, to
be one with their purpose, but free from
their inadequacy, to fulfill what they only
propose, to attain what they only will.   In
saying this I in no sense mean that reality
meets all your momentary wishes and caprices.   For your momentary wishes and
caprices are simply unconscious of their
own whole meaning ; and therefore they
very generally have to be transformed in
order to be satisfied.   But what my doctrine does mean is that a world of ontological fragments, of facts that are not in
one whole of meaning together, is never
to be found.   There are no ideas sundered
from their objects.   Ontologically speaking, where the idea is, there is the object
also.   Only the momentary human idea is
the object imperfectly brought to a finite
consciousness.   The apparent sundering of
idea and fact is therefore simply an illusion

of our own finitude. Nor do the ideas
mysteriously refer to objects that first exist
beyond them and *then* are somehow the
topics of this reference. No, the true
relation of idea and object is not mysterious. It is merely the very relation so
familiar to any of us, the relation which
you have now in mind when you observe
that you have not fully present to your
momentary self the fulfillment of your own
present conscious purposes, nor yet a full
consciousness even of what those purposes
themselves mean. In fact, just in so far
as you lack anything, or in so far as you
know not wholly what you mean, or have
not now what you all the while consciously
seek, just in so far you define your object
as beyond you. The incompleteness of
your present self-expression of your own
meaning is then the sole warrant that you
have for asserting that there is a world
beyond you. And this incompleteness, so
far as you are conscious of it, gives in its
turn the only possible meaning to the ex-

ternality ascribed to the complete expression of your present meaning. Thus while you indeed expect reality to defeat your caprices, and to refute your errors, you still rightly demand that reality should adequately express your whole true meaning.

In consequence, merely by reading this result in the reverse order you have at once a definition of the deepest essence of the existent world. What is real is simply, in its wholeness, that which consciously completes or finally expresses the very meaning that, in you, is at this instant of your human experience consciously incomplete. That meaning of yours, viz., the world, the reality, the whole, yes the absolute, is now in its very being really although inadequately present to you passing consciousness ; but your finite defect is that you know not consciously, just now, the whole of what you even now genuinely mean. Or again : you have not now at once both wholly and consciously present

the complete expression of your own will. But this complete expression, with you and in essence in you really, even now, but not consciously present to you now, this whole will and life of yours is the world. That complete expression, as the Hindoos said, — *that is the Reality, that is the Soul, that art Thou.* The real world then is teleological. It does express a purpose. It does express this purpose rationally, wholly, finally. And this purpose is the very purpose now hinted in your own passing thrill of hope and of longing.

V

UT now, after listening to this mere
sketch of the general idealistic
theory of the ultimate reality, after
hearing this interpretation of the essential
nature of the world order in its wholeness,
you may well ask how, in case there is this
essential relation of every finite idea to the
whole meaning of the world, there is any
room left for finite individuality as any distinguishable fact.   The doctrine that I have
just sketched is indeed obviously a version
of a doctrine about God as an Absolute
Being, and about his relation to every finite
conscious life just in so far as that life,
seeing its own imperfections, is seeking
for truth beyond itself.   No one can seek
for a truth beyond his present self, unless
the seeker is already in his inmost purpose
one with the Absolute Life in which all

truth is expressed. But on the other hand, this oneness of divine and of finite purpose is in some sense sure to exist in case of every finite life; for all life is an expression of the one universal Will, and in its turn is in the most intimate relation to that one will. Ignorance and error as well as evil are, when viewed as such, and in their separation from the whole, imperfect self-expressions of the Absolute that can only appear within the limits of a finite fragment of the whole, such as any one of us now is. No finite idea can fail, even in the lowest depths of its finitude, to intend this oneness with the Absolute upon which, according to our account, all knowledge and all truth depend. But on the other hand, if all reality is one and for One, and is the expression of a single purpose, so that God is immanent, is everywhere nigh to the finite life, and is everywhere meant by us all, — then we seem indeed to have found that the world expresses one absolute purpose, and is real only as accomplishing

that purpose. And we seem to have found also that at any instant what we consciously intend, in all our finite strivings, is oneness with God. But what, you may ask, has become of our individuality, in so far as we were to be just ourselves, and nobody else?

I reply, first, that in referring to reality in these idealistic terms, as the final fulfillment of a united purpose, — as the complete carrying out of what all finite purposes more or less blindly intend, — we have at least pointed out where there is attained something which no abstract description of finite facts could show us, namely, the uniqueness of the Divine Life, and of the real world in which this life is expressed. A will satisfied has in God's whole life found its goal, and seeks no other. I do not indeed conceive the Absolute as finding his goal at any one point in what we call time. Now we wait and suffer and seek. And all life, all striving, and all science are efforts to win ultimately this

absolute meaning, which is our own will completely expressed. But it is the whole world of past, present, and future, it is that totality of life and of experience which our every moment of conscious life implies and seeks, which is fulfilled in the Absolute.[6] Now neither abstract thought nor immediate experience, taken merely as we men find or define them, can describe or discover the unique. Only the complete fulfillment of purpose can leave no other fact beyond to be sought; and primarily, for this very reason, only the Absolute Life can be an entirely whole individual. God, then, is indeed the primary individual. His world, his life, his expression taken in its wholeness, is that individual fact which you and I are at all times trying to find, to win, to see, to describe, to attain. As finite beings we fail at every moment. It is our failure that we try to correct by our science or by our prudence. By no mystic vision can we win our union with him. We must toil. But he is our whole true life, in whom

we live and move and have our being, and in him we triumph and attain, — not now, not here in time and amidst the blind strivings of this instant, but in that which our strivings always intend, and pursue, and love. For " restless are our souls," as Augustine in the familiar passage said, "until they rest, O God, in thee."

But now, on the other hand, consider the consequences of all this for ourselves. The two deepest facts about the real world are, from this idealistic point of view, that it is everywhere the expression, more or less partial and fragmentary, of meaning and of purpose. Therefore it makes our science and our practical work possible, and demands them of us. But if viewed as a whole it is an unique fulfillment of purpose, — the only begotten son of the Divine Will. It is such then, in its wholeness as a God's world, that nothing else could take its place consistently with the will which the whole freely expresses, carries out, and fulfills. But now of an unique whole, every

fragment and aspect, just by virtue of its relation to the whole, is inevitably unique. Were the world essentially unfinished, and were it not the expression of a purpose, then the uniqueness or individuality of any of its parts or aspects would remain a fact nowhere present to anybody's insight. But if the absolute knowledge sees the whole as a complete fulfillment of purpose, then every fact in the world occupies its unique place in the world. Were just that fact changed, the meaning of the whole would be just in so far altered, and another world would take the place of the present one. Just as, in case a given cathedral is unique, and has not its equal in all the world of being, then every stone and every arch and every carving in that cathedral is unique, by having its one place in that whole, just so too, in the universe, if the whole is the expression of the single and absolute will, every fragment of life therein has its unique place in the divine life, — a place that no other fragment of life could fill.[7]

And so, although you can never see, and can never abstractly define, your own unique or individual place in the world, or your character as this individual, you are unique and therefore individual in your life and meaning, just because you have your place in the divine life, and that life is one. And therefore it is true that in this same realm of the single divine life which loves and chooses this world as the fulfillment of its own purpose, and will have no other, your friend's life glows with just that unique portion of the divine will that no other life in all the world expresses. We finite beings then are unique and individual in our differences, from one another and from all possible beings, just because we share in the very uniqueness of God's individuality and purpose. We borrow our variety from our various relations to his unity.

And thus the claims of Knowledge and of Will are from the absolute point of view reconciled. For knowledge recog-

nizes no diversity except upon the ground
of an identity. And this is true of us all,
— namely, that our very variety is based
upon the fact that the absolute life and its
world form one whole and are in their oneness unique. For just because the satisfied divine purpose permits no other to
take the place of this world, in its wholeness, just so each one of us has his own
distinct place in this unique whole. But
on the other hand Will primarily seeks
that which is different from all other objects, — namely, the individual, the finality,
the single fulfillment of striving. And just
such a fact is the whole world, and therefore is every part thereof unique in its own
kind and degree of being.

VI

O far, then, as we live and strive
at all, our lives are various, are
needed for the whole, and are
unique. No one of these lives can be
substituted for another. No one of us
finite beings can take another's place.
And all this is true just because the Universe is one significant whole.

That follows from our general doctrine
concerning our unique relation, as various
finite expressions taking place within the
single whole of the divine life. But now,
with this result in mind, let us return again
to the finite realms, and descend from our
glimpse of the divine life to the dim shad-
ows and to the wilderness of this world,
and ask afresh: But *what* is the unique
meaning of my life just now? What place
do I fill in God's world that nobody else
either fills or can fill?

How disheartening in one sense is still the inevitable answer. I state that answer again in all its negative harshness. I reply simply : For myself, I do not now know in any concrete human terms wherein my individuality consists. In my present human form of consciousness I simply cannot tell. If I look to see what I ever did that, for all I now know, some other man might not have done, I am utterly unable to discover the certainly unique deed. When I was a child I learned by imitation as the rest did. I have gone on copying models in my poor way ever since. I never felt a feeling that I knew or could know to be unlike the feelings of other people. I never consciously thought, except after patterns that the world or my fellows set for me. Of myself, I seem in this life to be nothing but a mere meeting-place in this stream of time where a mass of the driftwood from the ages has collected. I only know that I have always tried to be myself and nobody else. This

mere aim I indeed have observed, but that is all. As for you, my beloved friend, I loyally believe in your uniqueness; but whenever I try to tell you wherein it consists, I helplessly describe only a type. That type may be uncommon. But it is not you. For as soon as described, it might have other examples. But you are alone. Yet I never tell what you are. And if your face lights up my world as no other can — well, this feeling too, when viewed as the mere psychologist has to view it, appears to be simply what all the other friends report about their friends. It is an old story, this life of ours. There is nothing new under our sun. Nothing new, that is, for us, as we now feel and think. When we imagine that we have seen or defined uniqueness and novelty, we soon feel a little later the illusion. We live thus, in one sense, so lonesomely here. For we love individuals; we trust in them; we honor and pursue them; we glorify them and hope to know them. But after

we have once become keenly critical and
worldly wise, we know, if we are sufficiently
thoughtful, that we men can never either
find them with our eyes, or define them in
our minds ; and that hopelessness of finding
what we most love makes some of us cyni-
cal, and turns others of us into lovers of
barren abstractions, and renders still others
of us slaves to monotonous affairs that
have lost for us the true individual meaning and novelty that we had hoped to find
in them.   Ah, one of the deepest tragedies
of this human existence of ours lies in this
very loneliness of the awakened critics of
life.   We seek true individuality and the
true individuals.   But we find them not.
For lo, we mortals see what our poor
eyes can see ; and they, the true individuals, — they belong not to this world of
our merely human sense and thought.

They belong not to this world, in so far
as our sense and our thought now show us
this world !   Ah, therein, — just therein lies
the very proof that they even now belong

to a higher and to a richer realm than ours.
Herein lies the very sign of their true immortality.   For they are indeed real, these
individuals.   We know this, first, because
we mean them and seek them.   We know
this, secondly, because, in this very longing
of ours, God too longs ; and because the
Absolute life itself, which dwells in our
life, and inspires these very longings, possesses the true world, and *is* that world.
For the Absolute, as we now know, all life
is individual, but is individual as expressing
a meaning.   Precisely what is unexpressed
here, then, in our world of mortal glimpses
of truth, precisely what is sought and longed
for, but never won in this our human form
of consciousness, just that is interpreted,
is developed into its true wholeness, is won
in its fitting form, and is expressed, in all
the rich variety of individual meaning that
love here seeks, but cannot find, and is
expressed too as a portion, unique, conscious, and individual, of an Absolute Life
that even now pulsates in every one of our

desires for the ideal and for the individual.
We all even now really dwell in this realm
of a reality that is not visible to human
eyes. We dwell there as individuals. The
oneness of the Absolute Will lives in and
through all this variety of life and love and
longing that now is ours, but cannot live
in and through all without working out to
the full precisely that individuality of purpose, that will to choose and to love the
unique, which is in all of us the deepest
expression of the ideal. Just because, then,
God is One, all our lives have various and
unique places in the harmony of the divine
life. And just because God attains and
wins and finds this uniqueness, all our lives
win in our union with him the individuality which is essential to their true meaning. And just because individuals whose
lives have uniqueness of meaning are here
only objects of pursuit, the attainment of
this very individuality, since it is indeed
real, occurs not in our present form of consciousness, but in a life that now we see

not, yet in a life whose genuine meaning is continuous with our own human life, however far from our present flickering form of disappointed human consciousness that life of the final individuality may be. Of this our true individual life, our present life is a glimpse, a fragment, a hint, and in its best moments a visible beginning. That this individual life of all of us is not something limited in its temporal expression to the life that now we experience, follows from the very fact that here nothing final or individual is found expressed.

HAVE had time thus only to hint at what to my mind is the true basis of a rational conception of Immortality. I do not wish to have the concrete definiteness of the prophecies which can be based upon this conception in the least overrated. Individuality we mean and seek. That, in God, we win and consciously win, and in a life that is not this present mortal life. But we also seek pleasure, riches, joys. Those, so far as they are mere types of facts, we as individuals have no right to expect to win, either here or elsewhere, in the form in which we now seek them. How, when, where, in what particular higher form of finite consciousness our various individual meanings get their final and unique expression, I also in no wise pretend to know or

to guess.   The confidence of the student
of philosophy when he speaks of the Absolute, arouses a curiously false impression
in some minds that he supposes himself
able to pierce further into all the other
mysteries of the world than others do.   But
that is a mistake.   I have had no time here
to give even to my argument for my conception of the Absolute any sort of exact
statement or defense.   I well know how
vague my hints of general idealism have
been.   I can only say that for that aspect
of my argument I have tried to give, in a
proper place, a fitting defense.

The case, however, for the present application of my argument to the problem of
Human Immortality lies simply in these
plain considerations : (1) The world is a
rational whole, a life, wherein the divine
Will is uniquely expressed.   (2) Every aspect of the Absolute Life must therefore
be unique with the uniqueness of the
whole, and must mean something that can
only get an individual expression.   (3) But

in this present life, while we constantly
intend and mean to be and to love and
know individuals, there are, for our present form of consciousness, no true individuals to be found or expressed with the
conscious materials now at our disposal.
(4) Yet our life, by virtue of its unity with
the Divine Life, must receive in the end a
genuinely individual and significant expression.   (5) We men, therefore, to ourselves,
as we feel our own strivings within us, and
to one another as we strive to find one
another, and to express ourselves to one
another, are hints of a real and various
individuality that is not now revealed to
us, and that cannot be revealed in any life
which merely assumes our present form of
consciousness, or which is limited by what
we observe between our birth and death.
(6) And so, finally, the various and genuine individuality which we are now loyally
meaning to express gets, from the Absolute point of view, its final and conscious
expression in a life that, like all life such
as Idealism recognizes, is conscious, and

that in its meaning, although not at all necessarily in time or in space, is continuous with the fragmentary and flickering existence wherein we now see through a glass darkly our relations to God and to the final truth.

I know not in the least, I pretend not to guess, by what processes this individuality of our human life is further expressed, whether through many tribulations as here, or whether by a more direct road to individual fulfillment and peace. I know only that our various meanings, through whatever vicissitudes of fortune, consciously come to what we individually, and God in whom alone we are individuals, shall together regard as the attainment of our unique place, and of our true relationships both to other individuals and to the all inclusive Individual, God himself. Further into the occult it is not the business of philosophy to go. My nearest friends are already, as we have seen, occult enough for me. I wait until this mortal shall put on — Individuality.

NOTES

NOTE 1, Page 5.

THE discussion of the problem of individuality in this lecture summarizes views that I have attempted to state and to defend at length in two places, viz., in the volume called *The Conception of God* (a discussion in which I took part with Prof. George H. Howison, Prof. Joseph LeConte, and Prof. Sidney E. Mezes: New York, The Macmillan Company, 1897; in particular, in the *Supplementary Essay*, *op. cit.*, pp. 217–326); and in the First Series of my Gifford Lectures before the University of Aberdeen (*The World and the Individual. First Series: The Four Conceptions of Being;* especially in lectures VII and X). The last mentioned volume is published by the Macmillan Company (1900).

NOTE 2, Page 21.

See Aristotle's *Physics*, I, 1. Aristotle mentions in this passage the language of children as illustrating his view.

NOTE 3, Page 33.

The technical justification for this assertion is only hinted later in the course of the present discourse, but is set forth at length in the discussions cited in Note 1. *The individual is essentially the object of an exclusive interest :* this is the thesis of the *Supplementary Essay* in *The Conception of God. All completely real Being is individual by virtue of the fact that it is a finally determinate expression of a purpose :* this is the doctrine defended in the Gifford Lectures (*loc. cit.*). The problem of the lover is, therefore, to my mind, as technically metaphysical a problem as is that of any theologian. His " exclusive interest " is a typical instance of the true principle of individuation.

NOTE 4, Page 39.

In this and in one or two other passages of the lecture the relation of the problem of the individual to the concept of the actual or completed Infinite is indicated. This aspect of the problem, involving as it does both mathematical and metaphysical issues, has received a somewhat detailed discussion in a *Supplementary Essay* published along with the first series of the Gifford Lectures, and entitled *The One, the Many, and the Infinite.*

It is in this connection that my own way of

stating the problem of individuality brings me into decided opposition to some well-known views, both of Fichte and of Hegel, regarding the nature of individuality and regarding the concept of the Infinite. An "elusive goal" the individual indeed is for any temporal search. Yet that in itself it is (in one sense, and that the most real sense) a completed whole, and not a *merely* unfinished process, is a central thesis of my whole argument. On the other hand, my concept of the completed Infinite is not that of Hegel, but rather that of Dedekind and Cantor.

NOTE 5, Page 50.

The more general statement of Idealism which follows, apart from its application to the case of the individual, is identical in substance with the argument set forth in my *Religious Aspect of Philosophy* (Boston, Riverside Press, 1885), and in my *Spirit of Modern Philosophy* (Id. 1892). In the Gifford Lectures the relation of the concept of Reality, as defined by Idealism, to the conceptions of Will and of Purpose, is more carefully considered than in the earlier discussions, and an attempt is made to show the precise grounds for the failure of the opposing conceptions of Being, *e. g.*, Realism.

NOTE 6, Page 65.

The text here implies a doctrine about the meaning of that much-abused term, Eternity. In the forthcoming second course of Gifford Lectures, already delivered but not yet printed, I have found the opportunity to state at length this doctrine, which is not new, but which has been far too much neglected in philosophical discussion. The gist of the matter may here be summed up in a few words. Whoever listens appreciatively to a melody, or to a sequence of chords of music, or even to a mere rhythm of drum-taps, or to the words of a speaker, has a twofold consciousness as to the way in which the facts to which he listens are *present* to him. (1) *Each* tone, or chord, or drum-tap, or spoken word, is *present*, as *this* member of its series, in so far as it *follows* some sounds and *precedes* others, so that when, or in so far as, in *this* sense, it is present, the preceding notes of the melody or taps of the rhythm are *no longer* or are past, while the succeeding notes are *not yet* or are future. In *this* sense of the term *present*, the present excludes past and future from its own temporal place in the sequence. (2) But now the appreciative listener also grasps *at once* (or, as a *totum simul*, to use the phrase of St. Thomas) the whole of a brief but still considerable sequence of tones or of taps or

of words. In this second sense he may be said to find *present* to him the whole sequence. How much he can thus grasp *at once* depends upon his interest, his temperament, and his training, but above all upon the characteristic *time-span* of human consciousness, or upon the length of what Professor James has, with others, called the "specious present." This length is, for us men, an arbitrary fact, varying more or less, but within close limits. It determines one aspect of what I have called the peculiar "form" of our human consciousness. What happens in periods too long or too short for this time-span of our consciousness escapes our direct observation. There is, however, no conceptual difficulty in the way of imagining a "form of consciousness" whose "specious present" should be limited in span to the time of vibration of a hydrogen molecule, or, on the other hand, should be extended to include in one glance, or *at once*, the events of a billion years. Such other forms of consciousness would be in no more arbitrary relations to time than our own consciousness now is. How we come to be able to grasp *at once* the events of say two or three seconds, we cannot now say. That we can do so is evidenced by every case in which we catch, as a presented fact, the interest of a whole musical or rhythmic or spoken phrase. Other forms of consciousness might have vastly different span.

But in so far as we grasp *at once* a whole series of facts, however long or however short, this series is present, in the *second* sense of the term *present*, to the consciousness that observes it as in any way a whole. Yet the temporal facts which make up the whole sequence follow each one *after* its predecessors. Let the sequence be *a*, *b*, *c*. Then, in our *first* sense of the term *present*, when *b* is present, *a* is *no longer*, and *c* is *not yet*. And this fact makes the temporal sequence what it is. But in the *second* sense of the term *present*, *a*, *b*, and *c*, despite this perfectly genuine but relative difference of *no longer* and *not yet*, or of *past* and *future*, are *all* present as a *totum simul* to the consciousness that grasps the entire sequence. These two senses of the term *present* are perfectly distinguishable, and they involve no contradiction.

Since, however, the length of a " specious present " is an arbitrary fact, there is no sort of contradiction in supposing a " form of consciousness " for which the events of the Archæan and of the Silurian and of later geological periods should be present *at once*, together with the facts of to-day's history. Such a consciousness would merely exceed, by many millions of years, our time-span ; but what is for us *no longer* would be, to such a consciousness, in our *second* sense of the term *present*, a fact of its own present consciousness. (On the time-

span, see also my discussion in my *Studies of Good and Evil*, published by Appleton and Company in 1898, in the essay entitled *Self-Consciousness, Social Consciousness and Nature*).

If all limitations of time-span are to be conceived as arbitrary, the question whether a consciousness is possible which should have present to it *at once* (in our second sense of the term *present*) the *whole of time*, or the whole of what, from *this* moment outwards, we now view as antecedent or as sequent to this moment, becomes simply the question, In what sense can the totality of temporal events be regarded as any determinate whole at all? This question involves, to be sure, the further questions: In what sense is the temporal sequence of the world's events an endless sequence or an infinite series? and, In what sense can this temporal series, even if infinite, be defined as a determinate or as a really complete whole? These questions lie far beyond the limits of this note. But, as a fact, in the above-cited essay, at the conclusion of the Gifford Lectures, on *The One, the Many, and the Infinite*, I have endeavored to show that an infinite series can be a perfectly determinate and individual whole, *every* member of which could conceivably be known *at once* by a single consciousness. For reasons that will be explained more fully in the second series of the Gifford Lectures, but that

are already indicated in the first series, I also hold
that the temporal series of the world's events constitutes such a whole, infinite, and yet present *at
once* to the Absolute (in our second sense of the
term *present*).

But a consciousness whose span embraces the
whole of time is precisely what I mean by the term
Eternal Consciousness. And what is present *at
once* to such a consciousness, viz., the whole of
what happens in time, taken together with all the
distinctions of past and of future that hold *within*
the series of temporal events, — this whole, I say,
constitutes *Eternity.* It is in these senses that I
here use these two terms.

The *type* of an eternal consciousness we ourselves
empirically possess precisely in so far as we grasp
at once the sequent events of any melody or rhythm
or series of words. This our possession of what
may be called the *eternal type* of consciousness is
limited by the arbitrary span of our human form of
consciousness. To conceive this limitation absolutely removed, without any confusion resulting,
implies, to be sure, the conception of the determi-
nately infinite whole; but this conception, although
abstruse, is (as I have tried to show in the essay
cited) a conception quite free from contradiction.
If once we form this conception, then it becomes
easy to see that to suppose the whole of time

present at once to an eternal consciousness is in no wise a meaningless supposition. Nor does this supposition conflict with the temporal truth that we also express when we say that, from the point of view of any one *present* event in time (if the term *present* is taken in our first sense), all future events are *not yet*, and all past events are *no longer*. The two propositions express different aspects of the world, but are mutually consistent.

It is in view of these considerations that the text speaks of the Absolute as possessing, in its conscious fulfillment, "the whole world of past and future." If one retorts, "How can the future *now*, *i. e.*, at the *present* moment, be *present* fact to the Absolute when the future is *not yet* ?" then I simply insist upon distinguishing the two foregoing meanings of the word "present." It is as if one asked, "How can the listener grasp at once as present the whole of his brief musical sequence, if the tones or chords so follow in time that *all but one* are either past or future, and are not present when that one sounds?" Whoever listens to music with appreciation answers the latter question. The answer to the former involves no new principle, if once you grant the definable reality of an infinite time.

The usual confusion of ideas as to this twofold way in which the facts of a sequence can be called

present is responsible for the familiar problem as to the divine "foreknowledge" and its relation to freedom. "If God has the future present to him, then he must *now* (viz., to-day, or at this temporal instant) *fore*know the future." So a frequently urged argument presupposes. The only fair comment is : God, viewed in his wholeness, does not *now* foreknow anything, if by *now* you mean merely *to-day* or *at this moment.* For whoever *now* looks forward to the future merely as *not yet*, is a finite being, temporally determined, and not yet come to his own fulfillment in God. Divine knowledge of what to us is future is no mere foreknowledge. It is eternal knowledge.

NOTE 7, Page 67.

I am well aware of the difficulty that this passage leaves wholly untouched regarding the sense in which there can be any freedom, any individual initiative, any ethical spontaneity, belonging to the individuals whose variety and uniqueness, despite, or even because of, their unity with and in God, is here asserted. The problem of individual freedom I have treated in the *Conception of God* (pp. 289–315), and in Lecture X of the first series of Gifford Lectures. See also *The Spirit of Modern Philosophy*, pp. 428–434. Fuller discussions of the same problem, already prepared in manuscript, will

appear in the second series of Gifford Lectures. I can only say that the figure of the cathedral is used in the text with a full consciousness of its inadequacy. The world is no cathedral, but a life of many lives. Nor are the true individuals mere stones or carvings in an edifice, nor yet mere parts in a quantitative whole. In God their lives interpenetrate without losing their contrasts, and are free despite their oneness. Their freedom involves the fact that the future temporal processes of the world have a certain measure of *causal* indeterminateness, despite that other, or ontological determinateness, that, as individual events, they possess; and that every temporal instant brings its own novelties with it. The completeness of their lives is a fact only from the eternal point of view. But a lecture on immortality is limited to the mere aspect of life and truth suggested by its title. It cannot justly express a system of metaphysics. It can only hint the nature of such a system.